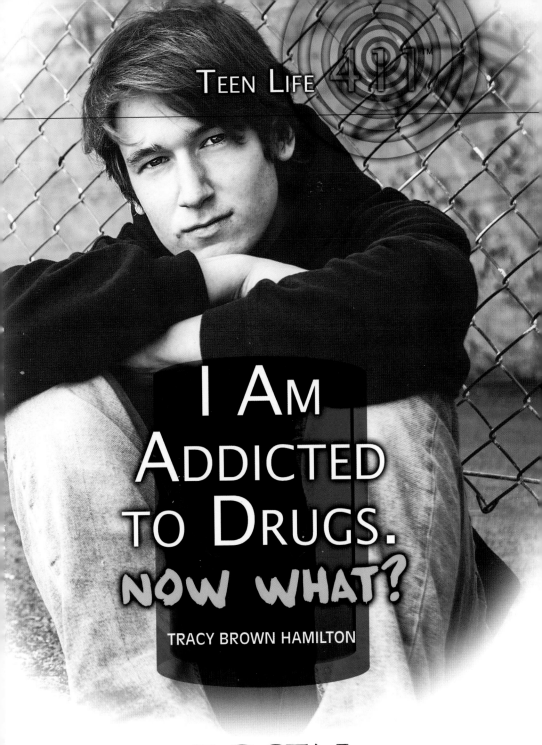

TEEN LIFE 411™

I AM ADDICTED TO DRUGS.
NOW WHAT?

TRACY BROWN HAMILTON

ROSEN
PUBLISHING®

Published in 2017 by The Rosen Publishing Group, Inc.
29 East 21st Street, New York, NY 10010

Copyright © 2017 by The Rosen Publishing Group, Inc.

First Edition

Library of Congress Cataloging-in-Publication Data

Names: Hamilton, Tracy Brown, author.
Title: I am addicted to drugs : now what? / Tracy Brown Hamilton.
Description: New York : Rosen Publishing, 2017. | Series: Teen life 411 | Includes bibliographical references and index.
Identifiers: LCCN 2016022733 | ISBN 9781508171980 (library bound)
Subjects: LCSH: Drug addiction–Treatment. | Drug addiction.
Classification: LCC RC566 .H35 2017 | DDC 362.29—dc23
LC record available at https://lccn.loc.gov/2016022733

Manufactured in Malaysia

CONTENTS

There is no end to the statistics existing on drug use in the United States. Here's a sampling from DoSomething.org: More teens die from prescription drugs than heroin/cocaine combined; In 2013, more high school seniors regularly used marijuana than cigarettes, as 22.7 percent smoked pot in the last month, compared to 16.3 percent who smoked cigarettes; 60 percent of seniors don't see regular marijuana use as harmful, but THC (the active ingredient in the drug that causes addiction) is nearly five times stronger than it was twenty years ago; one-third of teenagers who live in states with medical marijuana laws get their pot from other people's prescriptions, and so on.

Other studies find more optimistic results. According to a 2014 Monitor the Future survey conducted by the National Institute on Drug Abuse, "drug use and attitudes among American 8th, 10th, and 12th graders continued to show encouraging news about youth drug use, including decreasing use of alcohol, cigarettes, and prescription pain relievers; no increase in use of marijuana; decreasing use of inhalants and synthetic drugs, including K2/Spice and bath salts; and a general decline over the last two decades in the use of illicit drugs."

Statistics are interesting to consider, but when you are confronted by drug addiction, things seem more complicated. Curiosity and experimentation are a part of life, particularly when you are young, but what do you do if you feel you are losing control of the choices you make?

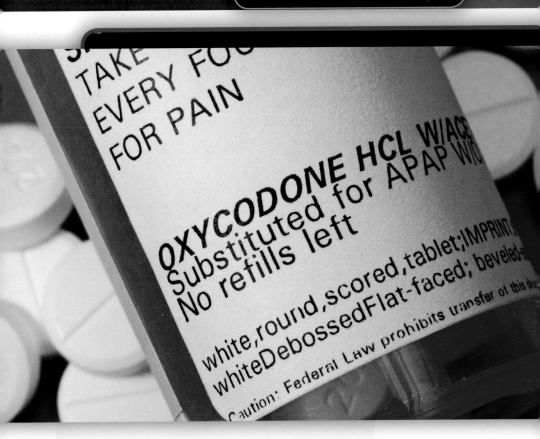

Many prescription drugs can be highly addictive. Rapper Eminem reportedly overcame a years-long addiction to Vicodin and Valium in 2010.

If recreational drug or alcohol use is starting to spiral out of control, if you feel like you are or may be becoming an addict, you need to seek help. But as a teenager, knowing what kind of help you need and where to find it can be complicated. Maybe your relationship with your parents or friends isn't such that they would be supportive and understanding. Maybe you're afraid of legal, social, or personal consequences if you reveal your addiction and seek help.

The aim of this book is to help the reader understand addiction—who can become an addict, how addiction works, and how to regain control and live drug free. It advises on how to handle the personal relationships that may be affected by drug use, or that may even be encouraging or enabling the addict to keep using.

You'll find information on what rehabilitation facilities are available, which one is right for you, and how rehab works. You'll also find strategies for the best chances of success in

Addiction may feel overwhelming to break, but you don't have to do it alone.

remaining sober after you've stopped using, including support groups that can help you avoid a relapse.

Drug addiction is a disease, and like any other, it is treatable. This book can help you get started on your recovery from addiction and help you get your life and your health back on track.

CHAPTER 1

HOW DO I KNOW IF I HAVE A PROBLEM WITH DRUGS?

Drugs are dangerous for many reasons. Even drugs that are legal, like alcohol, or prescribed by your doctor, like pain killers, can do a lot of harm to your health and mind-set. Addiction is one of the ways drug use can turn from recreational or therapeutic into a painful—but recoverable—predicament.

It is difficult for many people to admit they are addicted to a substance. Some people are afraid to acknowledge they have a problem because they don't want their friends or family to judge them or consider them weak. Others deny their addiction because they don't feel ready to give up the drug for fear of having to live without it.

Coming to terms with an addiction is the first step in correcting the problem, freeing yourself from the addiction, and getting on with a healthier, happier life. To do that, you need to be able to recognize the problem and understand more about what addiction is, what its root causes are, and how addiction works.

Many addicts begin using drugs and alcohol as a means to unwind or have fun but then lose control over their desire for the substance.

What Is Addiction?

Addiction is a disease, rather than a sign of weakness or irresponsibility. That can be difficult to understand, because a lot of drug use starts out recreational or experimental, and many people assume they can just stop when they decide they have enough.

For many people, controlling the amount of a substance they use and stopping when they want to is indeed possible. Some people can have the occasional drink without any concern, for example. However, when people have an addiction, they lose control over the substance and can find they are unable to stop or control the amount that they take.

This happens because the addict's brain has been changed by recurrent use of a drug so that the person can't simply stop using the substance, even if they decide they want to. An addiction actually changes the way the addict's mind works, making them believe they need the drug to function.

Therefore, an addicted person becomes consumed with procuring and using the drug. It can become a higher priority than sleeping, eating, working out, maintaining relationships, or going to school or work. An addicted person will find he or she continues to seek the drug, despite the

Struggling with addiction can feel quite isolating, as many addicts have trouble admitting to themselves or others that they have a problem.

obvious negative impact it is having on things the person used to otherwise value.

Addiction can be physical; the addict's body can become so used to the drug being in their system that they no longer feel the same effects as they used to, but can feel unwell if the drug is absent from their bodies.

Addiction can also be mental if the brain is triggered by certain cues to want the drug. For example, if a person associates drinking or taking drugs with particular situations, being in that situation can trigger a very strong, perhaps irresistible, desire for that drug.

Addictive substances do not discriminate based on gender or race. Anyone who uses a drug even just a few times can become an addict.

It could be something like a beer at parties or some marijuana after a long day.

Scientists used to believe that addiction was a simple matter of poor moral values or lack of discipline, but now the medical community knows a lot more about how it works. Repeated usage of an addictive drug actually alters the way your brain communicates between the area that drives us to do something, and the part that connects liking something with needing it. This is what it means to be addicted: to be consumed with continuing to use a substance that your brain tells you to pursue, despite the negative consequences.

Who Can Become an Addict?

Who can become an addict? In short, anyone. Anyone at any age, of any race, religion, nationality, sex, or income level can become addicted to a substance.

Research has identified groups of people who are, at least statistically, more likely to have problems with addiction—but this doesn't mean it can't happen to anyone.

According to the Closing the Addiction Treatment Gap (CATG) initiative nearly twenty-three million Americans—that's almost one in ten—are addicted to alcohol or other drugs. Marijuana, opioid painkillers, and cocaine are the top three drugs people become addicted to, and more than two-thirds of all addicts also abuse alcohol alongside of other drugs.

Men between eighteen and twenty-four years old, for example, are more likely to become addicts than women. And, although African American males are arrested at a rate ten times higher than white males for drug crimes, a 2012 National Survey on Drug Use and Health, based on data from 72,561 youth interviews, found that African Americans are actually less likely to develop addictions.

The study found that 15 percent of Native American youths had the highest chance of getting a substance abuse disorder, compared to 9 percent of Caucasians, 5 percent of African Americans, and 3.5 percent of Asian Americans.

There is no way to absolutely predict how much of a substance a person takes or how frequently they use before they can become addicted. Not everybody who uses a drug abuses the drug, but it's difficult to know who will be susceptible—which is why it's always best to avoid taking the drug in the first place.

Why Do Some People Become Addicts, and Others Not?

According to some studies, there are some factors that are shown to make some people more vulnerable to addiction than others. They involve your genes—is there a history of addiction in your family?—as well as your social environment. Researchers also find that the younger you start using, the more likely it is that an addiction will form.

HelpGuide.org lists the factors that increase your vulnerability to addiction as:

- Family history of addiction
- Abuse, neglect, or other traumatic experiences
- Mental disorders such as depression and anxiety
- Early use of drugs
- Method of administration—smoking or injecting a drug may increase its addictive potential

Scientists talk about a so-called "addiction gene," which means they are looking for biological factors—traits inherited from your parents—that might make it harder for some people to quit taking a drug once they start. Your genes can also affect how you will physically respond to a drug.

A drug that makes some people feel euphoria or extreme pleasure might make another person physically ill. An addiction gene is not a specific gene but more a series of genes, which may cause a person to be more likely to become an addict.

However, your genes do not make it impossible to recover from an addiction. They are indicators of the likelihood of your developing one, but anyone can kick an addiction and recover, regardless of their genes or family history of addiction.

Michael Phelps, swimmer and winner of twenty-eight Olympic medals, was suspended from swimming after driving drunk in 2014. He has since recovered from his addiction.

Many famous people—actors, musicians, athletes—have suffered drug addiction but dealt with the problem, achieved sobriety, and got their careers and personal lives back on track. Recovery is possible. Here are just a few people who can prove it, according to drugabuse .com.

- **Michael Phelps:** After a second driving under the influence (DUI) arrest, Olympic swimmer Michael Phelps checked into rehab in 2014 to deal with his alcohol problem.
- **Drew Barrymore:** Actress Drew Barrymore was in rehab twice by the age of thirteen after having her first drink at age nine, smoking marijuana at ten, and doing cocaine at twelve.
- **Britney Spears:** Pop singer Britney Spears entered rehab in 2006 after rumors of drug addiction threatened her career.
- **Mary-Kate Olsen:** Actress Mary-Kate Olsen suffered with anorexia and cocaine addiction and eventually got better through rehab.
- **Robert Downey Jr.:** Actor Robert Downey Jr. was notorious for his drug and alcohol abuse and is now one of the most inspiring examples of recovery.

Celebrities Who Fought from Addiction to Recovery

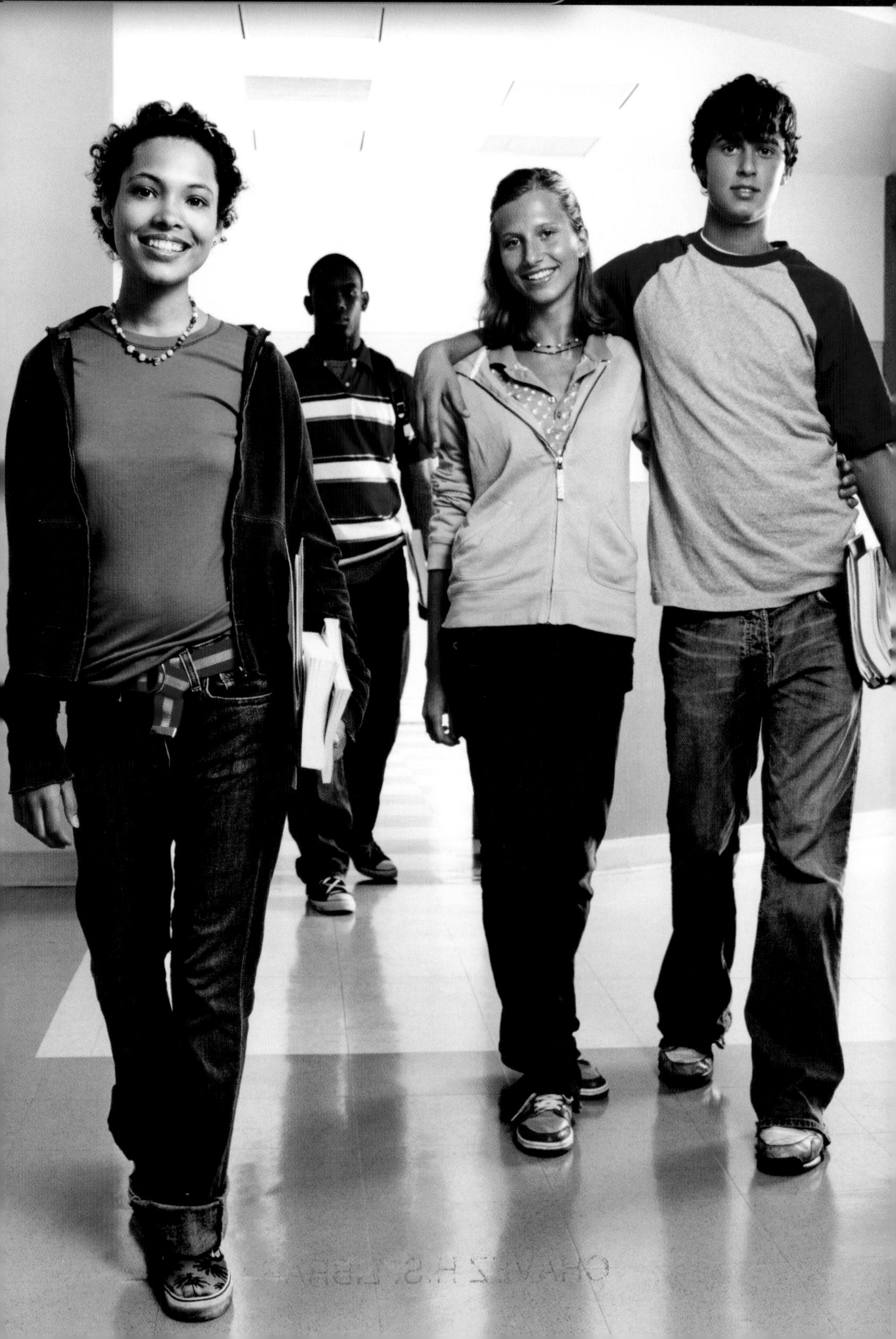

How Do I Know if I'm an Addict?

Alcoholics Anonymous (AA) is an alcohol addiction recovery program—its site calls itself a "fellowship"—that helps alcoholics recover. It is based on a twelve-step program, the first step of which is "admitting you have a problem."

This is true for all addictions—alcohol, drugs, gambling, sex, and so on: you first have to identify and accept that you have lost control over your desire for or use of something that you identify with pleasure.

The question of whether you are an addict is a difficult and sometimes confronting one, and it's a question only you can answer. You have to be very honest with yourself about your drug use and how much control you have over it.

Wondering whether you have a drug addiction is a good indication that you may have a developing dependency. One way to check whether your drug usage has begun the slippery slope from recreational or medicinal usage to full blown addiction is to abstain for a period of time, see how you feel, and whether you find it difficult coping with sobriety. Of course, the best thing to do is quit using the substance completely.

Addiction doesn't play favorites. Anyone can be at risk.

Think You Might Be an Addict? Answer These Questions

Narcotics Anonymous (NA) describes itself as a "non-profit fellowship or society of men and women for whom drugs had become a major problem." Here are the questions NA suggests people who wonder if they have a problem ask themselves and seek honest answers to.

1. Do you ever use alone?
2. Have you ever substituted one drug for another, thinking that one particular drug was the problem?
3. Have you ever manipulated or lied to a doctor to obtain prescription drugs?
4. Have you ever stolen drugs or stolen to obtain drugs?
5. Do you regularly use a drug when you wake up or when you go to bed?
6. Have you ever taken one drug to overcome the effects of another?
7. Do you avoid people or places that do not approve of you using drugs?
8. Have you ever used a drug without knowing what it was or what it would do to you?
9. Has your job or school performance ever suffered from the effects of your drug use?
10. Have you ever been arrested as a result of using drugs?

11. Have you ever lied about what or how much you use?
12. Do you put the purchase of drugs ahead of your financial responsibilities?
13. Have you ever tried to stop or control your using?
14. Have you ever been in a jail, hospital, or drug rehabilitation center because of your using?
15. Does using interfere with your sleeping or eating?
16. Does the thought of running out of drugs terrify you?
17. Do you feel it is impossible for you to live without drugs?
18. Do you ever question your own sanity?
19. Is your drug use making life at home unhappy?
20. Have you ever thought you couldn't fit in or have a good time without drugs?
21. Have you ever felt defensive, guilty, or ashamed about your using?
22. Do you think a lot about drugs?
23. Have you had irrational or indefinable fears?
24. Has using affected your sexual relationships?
25. Have you ever taken drugs you didn't prefer?
26. Have you ever used drugs because of emotional pain or stress?
27. Have you ever overdosed on any drugs?
28. Do you continue to use despite negative consequences?
29. Do you think you might have a drug problem?

CHAPTER 2

WHY CAN'T I DO IT ALONE? I KEEP TRYING TO STOP.

Why don't addicts just stop? This is a question people have asked for generations. It goes against logic to put something into your body that negatively affects your health, energy level, chances for success in school, sports or whatever activities you care about, social life, and relationship with your family.

For many reasons, it's not that simple to just stop. Recovering from addiction is not simply about quitting drugs, or just a matter of not doing something—it's a more active process than that. You have to have a plan for sobriety. You have to have a support structure around you strengthening your chances of living without the drug instead of falling back into the trap of addiction.

The very word "addiction" comes from the Latin for "enslaved by" or "bound to." It becomes more than a choice to take the drug, which means it takes more than making a choice to stop.

There are many social and physical aspects to addiction that make it very hard to quit and stay drug free. This chapter explores what some of these are and how they can be overcome to win the battle against addiction.

IT'S ALL IN YOUR HEAD

Many studies have been done on how various drugs affect your brain while you are under the influence—how marijuana shuts down neurons in your brain that tell you you're full, hence many pot smokers often feel hungry; how alcohol releases dopamine making a drinker feel more relaxed and with lowered inhibitions;

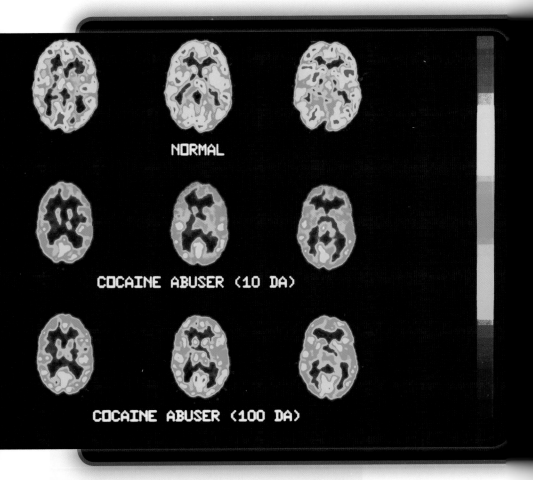

NORMAL

COCAINE ABUSER (10 DA)

COCAINE ABUSER (100 DA)

Some of the changes that the drug cocaine will cause to various parts of a user's brain can be seen on these brain scan images.

how cocaine leads users to make bad decisions because it affects a part of the brain that normally helps us learn from mistakes.

Some of these effects wear off as soon as a user is sober again. But there are also long-lasting changes that occur in the brain when a substance is used heavily over a period of time, and that leads to the brain disease of addiction.

Simply put: addiction hijacks your brain. The National Institute on Drug Abuse defines drug addiction this way:

> *Addiction is defined as a chronic, relapsing brain disease that is characterized by compulsive drug seeking and use, despite harmful consequences. It is considered a brain disease because drugs change the brain; they change its structure and how it works. These brain changes can be long lasting and can lead to many harmful, often self-destructive, behaviors.*

When your brain is exposed over time to a particular substance, it is altered to believe that it needs that substance in order to function properly. That is why it is so hard for an addict to just stop: the brain is telling an addict that it needs a substance and that seeking it out is

Trying to take control of an addiction on your own just by deciding to stop is very difficult because of the way drugs alter your brain.

the top priority for survival. It is very difficult to fight with your own brain.

Here's how Dr. Scott Glassman, clinical assistant professor and associate director of the mental health counseling program at the Philadelphia College of Osteopathic Medicine, explains it:

> There is a part of the brain closely tied to addictive behavior called the nucleus accumbens, or "reward center." Activity in this area is related to how much a person wants something. Anything that is pleasurable can increase activity in the nucleus accumbens, and lead to an addiction (food, gambling, video games, etc.)
>
> Stimulant drugs like cocaine and amphetamines cause increases in dopamine, which enhances excitement, alertness, activity, and mood. As a result of repeated stimulant drug use, this brain structure is increasingly able to release dopamine, and leads to increased desire for the drug. At the same time, the nucleus accumbens stops responding to other incentives, and filters out other more traditional signals that help us find activities rewarding. Individuals, as a result, find more and more of their lives devoted to pursuing the drug.

Shame Can Keep You Using

If you had a broken leg, you would go to the doctor and get a cast. If you had the flu, you would get medicine for it. If you had cancer, you would seek treatment. These are all medical issues that carry no stigma or shame: you have a problem that needs medical attention, you get it. It's obvious.

Yet many addicts, or drug abusers, are embarrassed or hesitant to admit they have a problem. Rather than let people know they no longer want to abuse a substance, they continue doing harm to themselves because they are ashamed to admit they can no longer just use a drug recreationally, especially if their friends don't seem to have a problem taking the occasional drink, for example.

People will surely notice if you are the only person no longer taking a drug, especially when others are indulging. What you tell them is up to you: you can say you don't like the feeling anymore, you can say you are trying to exercise or study more, or you can say you are concerned that you have become addicted.

Everyone has a right to their privacy, but you also have to put your health and happiness above all other issues if you want to recover fully. Whatever you tell people, the important thing is to stick to your resolve and not let others convince you that your drug use is no big deal if you think it is.

I Don't Want to Lose My Friends

A more long-term solution, and certainly one that offers a higher chance of success, is to break away from circumstances or friends centering on drug use. Triggers

are people, places, or situations that can intensify the desire to use a drug. Avoiding triggers makes it easier for an addict to find new outlets for pleasure or socializing.

You can try to find sober activities to do with your friends; let them know you are no longer interested in using drugs, but would still like to hang out with them in another way.

If they don't respect this or if you find there's not much more you have in common when sober, you probably need to get yourself some new friends. Think about what you like doing, what your true interests are, and seek out people who like those things, too.

Addiction can make you feel helpless and lonely. But if your friends want to keep using, they're not the friends you need.

There's an expression that addicts don't have friends, just accomplices. Many drug users feel betrayed if the person they used to do the drug with suddenly wants to stop. They might be afraid they will need to stop, too, and they are not ready. Intentionally or not, this can make friends lure you back into using a drug, and for that reason it's best for you to move on.

Fear of Living Sober

This chapter has discussed many of the hurdles an addict faces to stop using. But perhaps the biggest one is simply not really wanting to stop. If you have found comfort or pleasure— even if only imagined comfort

To succeed at ending a drug habit, a recovering addict has to make many lifestyle changes to avoid temptation or relapse.

and pleasure—using a drug, it can be very easy to convince yourself that you are better off continuing to take the drug.

And facing life without the drug can be very scary. Although making the decision to stop taking a drug and managing to actually stop are very difficult and major steps, many people find that not everything falls right back into place in their lives once they are sober.

Drug use is typically a symptom of other problems that don't automatically go away when the drug use stops. It's challenging to confront life without drugs once you've made them an escape mechanism. It

If a drug or alcohol habit has been an important part of your life for some time, it can be difficult at first to replace the habit with new activities.

requires working hard to rebuild relationships, to get back on track at school, to undo damage that has been caused by drug use, and to create a new framework for dealing with stress without escaping into drugs.

Looking at the Effects of Drugs on Your Brain

To understand how drugs change your brain, it helps to have some understanding of the parts of the brain that are most affected. Drugs affect three main areas of the brain, according to DrugAbuse.org:

The brain stem: This part of your brain controls the main functions that keep you alive, such as breathing and digesting. It is connected to your spinal cord, which moves your muscles and limbs, and it reports back to your brain what your body is doing.

The limbic system: This is a system of connections of brain structures. It is this part of your brain that controls emotional responses to stimuli, such as enjoying eating something delicious. The good feelings motivate us to repeat behaviors, or avoid them if they were unpleasant.

The cerebral cortex: This accounts for about three quarters of the human brain. It's divided into four areas, called lobes, which control specific functions, such as our senses. Some areas process information from our senses, allowing us to see, feel, and hear, and affect our ability to think, problem solve, and plan.

In recent years, the term "addict" has come under fire by people who believe the term stigmatizes people who struggle with drug dependency, making the problem a shameful one and therefore less understood by both drug users and those who live among them. Others argue that true "addiction" and therefore "addicts" don't exist; a person can be taught to have a different relationship with drugs and alcoholic (versus the argument that "once an addict, always an addict").

Blogger Johann Hari addressed this issue in a piece written for the *Huffington Post*. "Lots of people hear the word 'addict' and they picture a homeless, shiftless vampire, poised to commit any crime to get their drug; or a person raging on a meth-binge. If you're triggering those mental pictures, you're not undoing stigma, they argue. You're reinforcing it."

Still, Hari thinks the term has worth because it describes something very real: "To me, saying addiction doesn't exist is like saying love, or grief, or anger don't exist. It is a very widespread human phenomenon, and the vast majority of people, when they hear the word, know what you mean. It's when you feel compelled to engage in a behavior, even though some part of you doesn't want to, and even when it has negative consequences in your life."

SHOULD WE RETHINK THE WORD "ADDICT"?

Myths and Facts

Myth

Drug addiction is about making bad choices. It is a completely voluntary behavior.

FACT

A person may start out trying a drug for fun or to experiment, but regular use of a drug can change your brain so that you cannot control your compulsion to take the drug, even when the results and consequences are bad.

Myth

Addicts have flawed characters and are not good people.

FACT

Addiction is a disease that can strike anyone, from any educational or economic background, any race or gender, and any age or nationality.

Myth

If you have tried to stop using a drug and have even sought treatment but can't, there is no way you will ever stop.

FACT

Many addicts have several attempts at quitting a drug before actually succeeding. If you have a relapse, just keep trying to quit. Everyone is capable of getting control of addiction, but it can take many times trying before you achieve it.

CHAPTER 3

It can be very hard as a teenager to feel you can express what you are feeling to your parents. In part, it's because it's a time in life when you want to figure things out for yourself and work out solutions on your own or with peers. It sounds like a cliché, but the teen years are full of confusion brought on by new experiences and feelings. It's easy to feel like you are isolated, or to feel embarrassed, or simply that nobody—especially your parents—will be able to relate to how you are feeling.

Throw into that the possibility of a drug addiction and, depending on the type of relationship you have with your parents, caregivers, or other significant adults in your life, being open about your concerns can be very difficult. Whether you are feeling intimidated, ashamed, or scared, letting the people who can help you the most know what is going on is the best thing to do. This chapter looks at some of the issues that may be preventing you from wanting to talk to your parents or another trusted adult, with the aim being to make you feel less uncomfortable talking about your drug use.

TALKING WITH YOUR DOCTOR: EVEN TEENS HAVE A RIGHT TO PRIVACY

Being a teenager, you may feel like you have no privacy, no rights, and no power to control anything in your own life. Curfews, school schedules, rules, principals, parents, and pressure from your own peer group make it difficult to feel you have any autonomy, that is, any voice in what you do or experience. But even people under eighteen have rights, including the right to privacy.

What that means regarding drug use is that your doctor is actually forbidden by law to

Having family support when recovering from an addiction increases your chance at success, but some parents may react angrily when first learning of the problem.

share everything you tell him or her to your parents. Talking to your doctor about drugs and addiction is a good choice, whether it's a therapist or a general practitioner.

Your doctors will respect your privacy while answering all kinds of questions—including about your health, about sex, and about drugs. Your doctor has the knowledge and experience to answer your questions and provide advice. You can be sure there is very little your doctor has not heard before; it's unlikely your doctor will be surprised by anything you ask or share.

Your doctor may ask you questions that are very personal or potentially embarrassing, but it's important to be honest with him or her in order to get the help you seek.

You can make an appointment to see your doctor, and perhaps even arrange to talk with him or her over the phone. Your parents do not need to know if you make such an appointment. You can also mention it to your doctor while visiting him or her for another reason that your parents do know about.

Doctors have an obligation to keep the details of your conversations private. A doctor will not call your parents and tell them what you've shared. The only time doctors can break this promise of confidentiality, or secrecy, is if you are in danger of seriously hurting yourself or if someone else is causing you harm. There are laws that dictate that doctors must reveal information if

If a parent or guardian is not in a position to support your recovery, reach out to another adult who can.

there is real danger that someone may be harmed, such as a suicide.

Your doctor can also help you reach out to your parents or guardian, if that is something you want to do but are unsure how to approach.

Consider That Your Parents May Help You

Everyone's relationship with his or her parents is different. Some teens have very open relationships that allow for conversations about everything and anything, free of judgment, shame, or fear. Other teens don't have that type of closeness with their parents and have reason to feel they can't reach out to them for help.

Most teens are in the middle. Perhaps you have a good enough relationship with your parents but have never had to confront them with anything really serious, such as drug use. Perhaps you feel unsure if they will react lovingly or angrily. Perhaps both. Some kids worry they will be sent away from their home, or punished harshly.

In general, parents became parents because they wanted to help raise their children to be healthy, happy adults. A drug addiction, like a cancer, is a medical problem. Not addressing it by not seeking treatment can be

An addiction can strain relationships with friends and family. When recovering, expect the healing of these relationships to take time and effort.

deadly. It can be difficult to navigate this problem on your own, so unless talking with your parents will endanger you, it's probably something worth considering very deeply.

It's possible they will be angry. It's likely they will want you to stop seeing your friends, and maybe they will give you stricter rules. But these are minor considerations compared with your mental and physical health.

Your parents may turn out to be your best emotional support. They may be the people who can find you the best recovery program and ensure that you keep on track with recovery after you stop using drugs. If you

Be sure anyone you reach out to for help with your addiction is trustworthy and will respect your desire for privacy.

are open with the people closest to you—those you live with and who love you—they can serve as a sort of "safety net" to make sure you are able to stop using and stay clean.

Being honest about your drug use might be a shock to your parents, but once they are able to adjust to and accept the facts, they can be your greatest ally in getting back on track with your health.

Do also understand that your parents may be doing their best, but their best may not, at first, be very good.

If you decide to talk with your parents, keep in mind that this is probably new territory for them. They may not automatically have the answers you need. They may not immediately respond as you hope they will. They may not know what to say, or they may react in a way that surprises you. They may blame themselves, they may threaten to throw you out, or they may even try to deny what you are saying to them. Give your parent some time to adjust to your news and space to consider what steps to take.

Look for Another Adult Who Can Help

If you feel sure your parents will not be supportive, or, if for another reason, you can't bring yourself to talk about your drug use with your parents, it's a good idea to consider reaching out to another adult. Although teens are quite capable and intelligent, adults have the life experience and connections to help you identify

How to talk to your parents about your drug use is a complicated topic. But what about how parents should talk to children about their own past drug use? In 2010, the *New York Times* ran a blog post that asked children and teenagers to share how they thought parents should share their experiences with drugs with their children. For the most part, commenters on the post said parents should be honest, but should not glorify their past drug use.

One commenter called Angelica, had this to say: "My father has discussed drugs and alcohol with my brothers and I. Without denying it, my dad told us direct that he has tried all different kinds of drugs when he was younger and that we shouldn't follow in his footsteps. I think that it is best that my dad told me straightforward rather than hiding it, then I will not learn the truth. Due to that, I believe that every parent should tell their children the truth about drugs and not hide it or deny it."

LOOKING AT IT ANOTHER WAY: HOW KIDS SAY PARENTS SHOULD TALK TO THEM ABOUT DRUGS

and find the help you seek, whether it's just someone to listen to you or to help you find a treatment facility.

Addiction recovery is very hard to go through secretly. If your parents are not an option, seek another adult to help you along the way.

This can be a teacher, a neighbor, the parents of a friend, an aunt or uncle, a coach, a doctor, a grandparent, an adult sibling or cousin, a religious leader—any adult you trust and who you know cares about you and has your best interest at heart.

Choose this person carefully. Be sure they will respect your privacy and not share the information with anyone else, including your parents. As with parents, an adult who cares about you may initially be surprised or even angry to hear about your drug use, but they will also be your best support and ally in getting back on track and staying off drugs.

Confronting your parents with your addiction may be scary for them, but they can be your strongest ally when it comes to quitting a dangerous habit.

Starting the Conversation with Your Parents About Drugs

If you decide to talk with your parents about drug use, whether you think you have a problem, worry about your friends, or just want to talk about the issue in general, it can be difficult to know how to go about starting the dialogue.

On its website, the CRC Health Corporation (CRC), a provider of substance abuse treatment services and youth treatment services in the United States, provides the following tips for starting the conversation with your parents about drugs.

• Do some research. The Internet is full of information about drug and alcohol abuse, teen treatment programs, and other resources. That way, if your parents aren't informed, at least you will be.

• Find the right time to talk. Wait until your parents are relaxed and can give you their undivided attention.

• Stay on topic. Don't let issues or resentments from a few weeks ago sidetrack you or your parents.

• Look for opportunities. If you're worried that bringing up the topic of drugs or alcohol will instantly make your parents assume you're doing it, wait for a TV commercial or news story to come on that addresses the topic, and start a conversation based around the story.

• Ask your parents about their adolescent years and what they learned about drug use.

Some parents might be afraid to admit to, for example, smoking pot or drinking heavily in their younger days, for fear that admitting it will be perceived as permission for their child to do the same. If your parents are open with you about their experience, be grateful for their insight and don't hold it against them. The more open you can both be, the better your relationship will be and the more you can support and help each other.

CHAPTER 4

WHAT KIND OF TREATMENT DO I NEED, AND WHAT'S OUT THERE?

They say recognizing you have a problem with drugs or alcohol is the first step to recovery. But then what? Treatment options are plentiful, thankfully, but that can also make it difficult to decide what type of treatment is best for you.

Successful treatment typically consists of several elements, including detoxification (the process by which the body rids itself of a drug), medication (depending on the drug an addict is using), behavioral counseling, and long-term strategies, such as help groups, for preventing relapse.

There are hospitals that treat addiction either on an in- or out-patient basis, meaning that you can either stay in the hospital for the length of your treatment, or you can visit the doctor during a set appointment as you would for any other illness.

There are support groups that meet in person and online. There are medications you can take, therapists you can see, and books you can read. Some people choose a combination of treatments. This is because addiction is not a simple fix. There are a lot of factors that go into becoming addicted, including

Recovering from an addiction on your own is very difficult, and you are more likely to relapse if you don't find some sort of recovery support group.

physical and psychological factors, as well as social and environmental. All of these need to be addressed in order to recover.

How Does Treatment Work?

The first step is often to address the physical issue of getting the drug out of your system safely. Some addicts suffer serious withdrawal symptoms that can make quitting "cold turkey," or simply just stopping taking the drug, very dangerous. If your body is used to ingesting a substance, cutting it off in one go without proper medical supervision can cause serious side effects and even death.

Psychological issues may also need to be dealt with, which is where therapy can help. Support groups can help keep you on track and expose you to a new circle of friends and acquaintances who share your struggle and goal to live drug free.

This chapter will explain the various options and types of treatment and the pro's and cons that exist for each. Of course, you should talk with your doctor and a trusted adult to help you determine what type of treatment is best for you.

Inpatient and Outpatient Rehab

Rehabilitation treatment, or rehab as it is commonly called, is what most people think of when they think about drug addiction treatment. It's in the news often: stars such as Lindsay Lohan, Demi Lovato, and Britney Spears have

Lindsay Lohan has found support for dealing with her substance abuse issues by going to rehab clinics.

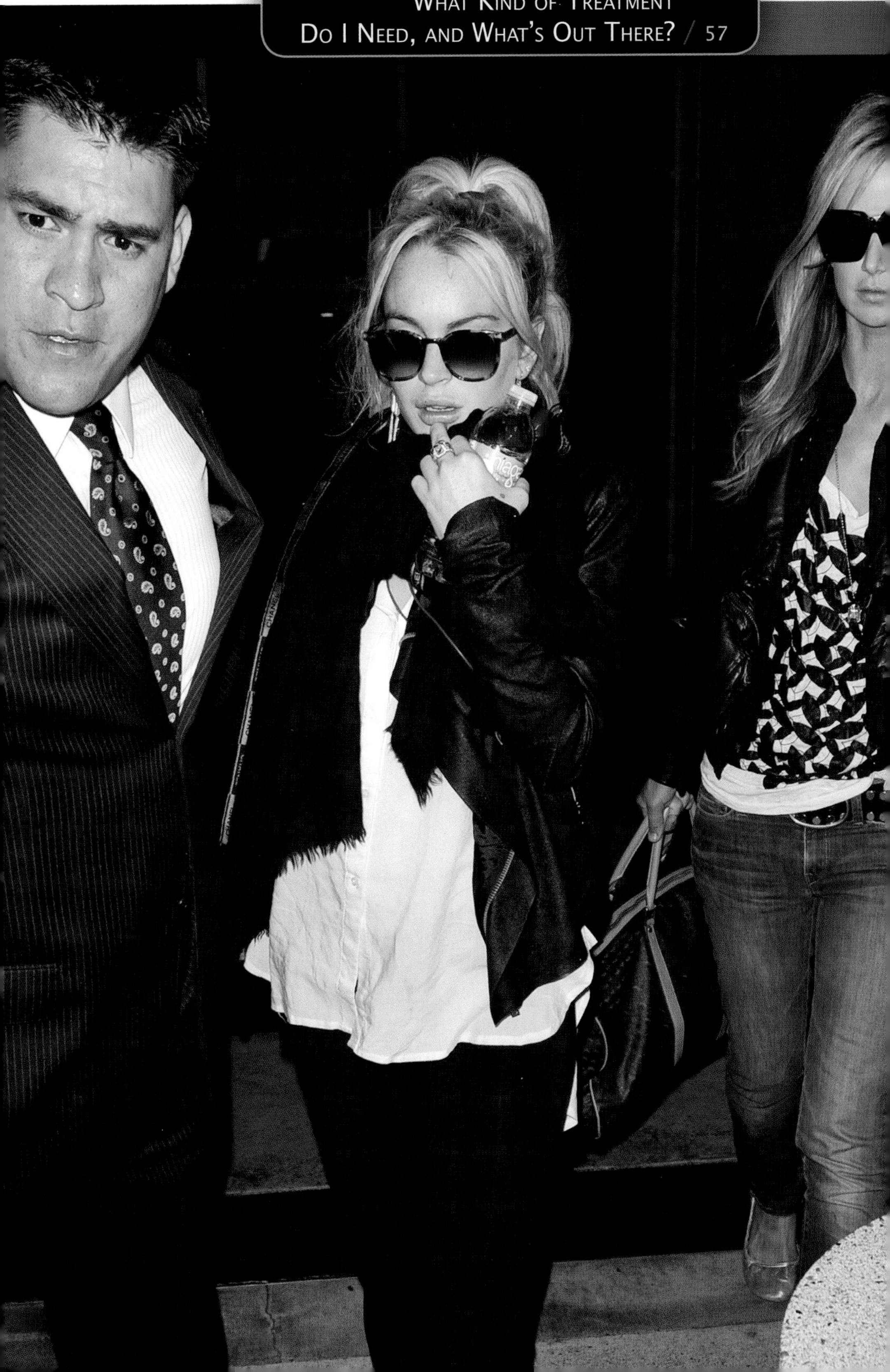

all checked in to a rehab facility at some point.

These inpatient rehab programs provide care to patients around the clock. Patients check in and live in the hospital for the duration of their treatment, which can be anywhere from twenty-eight to ninety days. This enables medical staff to observe patients and ensure they are not suffering from dangerous withdrawal symptoms. It also gives patients a chance to get away from their daily routines and living situations and away from any people or places that might trigger the desire to use.

Inpatient care generally includes group and private therapy sessions where patients can share their experiences, concerns, and challenges, as well as their goals for treatment and plans for maintaining sobriety after their time in the facility is over. These clinics often have other healthy activities for patients, anything from yoga to religious services, as desired.

Finding new ways to relax without drugs is a great way to prevent a relapse. Meditation has been found to be effective against addiction and depression.

For some people, however, it's not realistic to go away for a few weeks while getting help. Maybe they have a job or a family or just don't want everyone to know they are going to rehab. It also warrants mentioning that inpatient clinics tend to be much more expensive that outpatient options, which is a factor for many. In order for people to be able to receive treatment while maintaining their everyday life, there are outpatient clinics.

Outpatient care recipients must check in every day (usually except weekends and holidays) at the clinic to receive medication or counseling. Otherwise,

Trained medical professionals won't judge you for your former lifestyle and will know the best ways to help you stay sober safely.

SUPPORT GROUPS

Support groups are wonderful tools for maintaining sobriety and a drug-free life once you are physically free of the drug. These groups enable people who have had problems, or are having problems, with drugs to share their struggle and experiences with each other.

Just knowing you are not alone in your situation can be a great relief. But these groups can also help keep a recovering addict focused on staying sober, because they give you a community of people who share the common goal of not relapsing, or going back to using.

Finding the most effective recovery approach for you is key to your success, be it talking therapy, medication, or support groups.

Some of these groups exist in person, meeting in specific locations around your city or town. Others are accessible online.

Narcotics Anonymous (NA) is the most known and widely accessible support group for drug addicts in treatment and recovery. It is similar to Alcoholics Anonymous, but it focuses on all kinds of drugs, not just alcohol. It's a twelve-step program, like AA, and includes steps such as admitting that you are powerless to control your addiction or compulsion, recognizing a higher power "as you understand it" that can give strength, reviewing the mistakes you've made in the past and, with the help of your sponsor, making amends for past mistakes and wrongs, learning how to live a new life free from old unhealthy habits and ways of behaving, and helping fellow drug addicts.

There is also an international organization, Secular Organizations for Sobriety (SOS), that applies a science-based, self-empowerment approach to recovery from drug and alcohol addiction.

SMART Recovery (Self-Management and Recovery Training) aims to help recovering addicts live drug-free through self-empowerment and self-directed change.

There are even support groups for specific drugs, including Cocaine Anonymous, Crystal Meth Anonymous, and Marijuana Anonymous.

Although there are differences in approach and philosophy with various support group programs, in general, they all emphasize sharing stories, supporting each other, and the assignment of a sponsor, someone

Amy Winehouse, a singer who became famous for hits including the sadly ironic "Rehab," died in her home in London in 2011.

She had suffered a very public addiction to drugs and alcohol but appeared to have been recovering after several visits to rehab facilities.

Maintaining your sobriety is as important and as challenging as becoming sober through treatment and detoxification. Success rates vary depending on the statistics, but many people relapse, sometimes a few times, before achieving long-lasting sobriety.

Regardless of how long you have stayed drug-free, using even just one time can set you back to the beginning and require you to go through the recovery process all over again.

In the case of Amy Winehouse, despite publicly stating she did not wish to die and working very hard to become sober and clean, she ended up dying of alcohol poisoning after not drinking for a period of time.

There is debate over whether the adage "once an addict, always an addict" is true. It's possible some people can reprogram their bodies to, for example, drink moderately again. But the risks are quite high and don't seem worth taking. Once you've achieved drug-free living, it's best for you and your health to keep it that way.

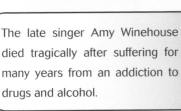
The late singer Amy Winehouse died tragically after suffering for many years from an addiction to drugs and alcohol.

THE DANGERS OF RELAPSE: AMY WINEHOUSE

you can contact whenever you want if you find yourself tempted to use.

Search online for programs in your area, or look for support groups that meet online. For example, HelloSundayMorning.org is an international community of people struggling with alcohol abuse or addiction.

No one understands your struggle better than a fellow recovering addict. Make use of support groups when you can.

CHAPTER 5

THE DRUG I USE IS ILLEGAL OR NOT LEGAL AT MY AGE. WILL I BE IN LEGAL TROUBLE?

While drug use and addiction are primarily health concerns, you can also find yourself in legal trouble if you are caught under the influence or in possession of a drug that is not legal, or not legal for you to use at your age.

This should not be confused with being in legal trouble if you are seeking help. If you confide in a doctor or an adult about your drug use, you should not worry that you will be in trouble with the law.

You should, however, be aware of the legal consequences that can occur if you are caught drinking underage or using, buying, selling, or carrying illegal substances. This chapter will look at the various laws that exist, particularly for minors, in regard to drugs.

HOW THE LAWS WORK

There are many substances that are controlled by laws, either state or federal laws, and these laws do apply to minors, or people under eighteen years of age.

People over eighteen are considered adults, and if they are caught in possession of illegal drugs, they are sent to trial court to face charges. Juveniles—people under eighteen—are sent to a different system, called the juvenile court system.

They are also referred to as juvenile delinquents, juvenile offenders, youthful offenders, or delinquent minors. The penalties for juveniles are different than from adults, but that doesn't mean they are not severe or without impact.

If, for example, you are caught with marijuana or methamphetamine by the police, and if they can prove you knew you had the drugs on your person, you can be charged with illegal drug possession. Be aware that even prescription drugs can lead to possession charges. A drug such as Oxycontin, an painkiller, is legal if the user has a prescription. It is not legal, however, to share the pills with anyone who does not have a prescription from their physician. Distributing such tablets is also illegal. Drinking is always illegal if you are under twenty-one years of age.

It's important to note that possession does not necessarily have to be in your pocket or in your backpack, or otherwise directly on your person. If drugs are found in your bedroom or you locker at school, for example, that can also lead to a possession charge.

A possession charge can lead to various consequences. Some of the outcomes that may result from an illegal drug possession charge include:

• Drug counseling: Juvenile courts typically focus on rehabilitating young people rather than punishing them, which is a good thing. A juvenile court can therefore

In addition to health and interpersonal problems, addiction can lead to difficulties with the law, and even jail time.

order an offender, and possibly his or her parents, to attend drug counseling.

• Probation: If a court puts an offender on probation, it means there are certain rules the juvenile must agree to and follow. This can mean attending school regularly, maintaining a job or finding one, going to drug counseling or family counseling, or performing community service. The court may also order the juvenile to regularly report to a juvenile probation officer or court officer. Probation lasts typically at least six months, but longer terms are possible.

• Diversion: Diversion is like probation, in that a juvenile on diversion must comply with specific court rules, but he or she does not have to formally go to court. If the juvenile successfully completes the diversion program, the charges are essentially dismissed.

• Detention: Sometimes, although it is rare, detention can result from a drug possession charge. This can mean home confinement, placement with a foster family or guardian, placement with a juvenile home, or placement in a juvenile detention center. This is typically reserved for more extreme cases, such as drug possession tied to a violent crime or in the case of repeat offenders.

A drug possession charge can have a lifelong impact and should be taken very seriously. A drug

If you are under eighteen and have a criminal record due to drug use, you may be able to have the record deleted depending on the laws in your state.

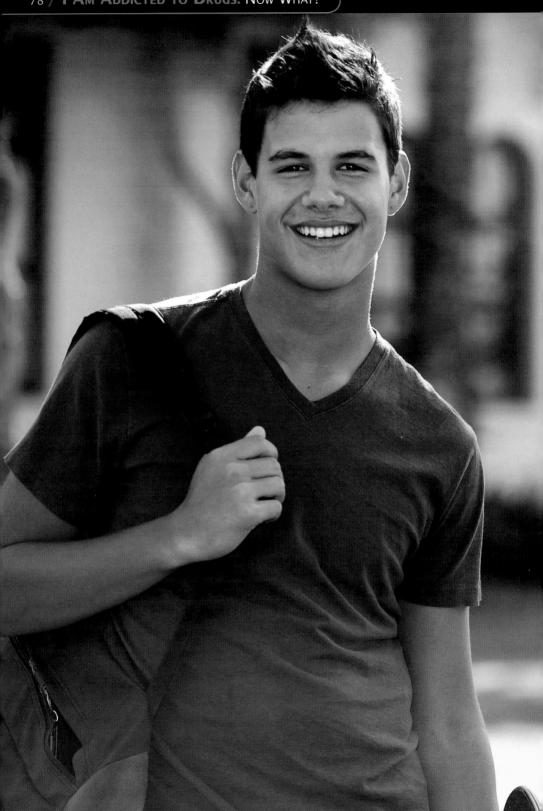

possession charge can ruin your chances to get a quality education, enter the military, or participate in school sports or other activities. It's always advisable to seek legal counsel—an attorney—in the case of legal issues relating to drug use.

GETTING RID OF A CRIMINAL RECORD

If you have a juvenile record, it is possible to have it expunged—erased, basically—which means you will not have to admit to it later in life, such as when applying for a job, to school, or for an apartment lease.

According to criminaldefenselawyer.com, the criteria for having your record expunged after you turn eighteen includes:

• Age: Some states provide for automatic expungement of certain juvenile records regardless of age but, usually, you must be an adult to have your record expunged. In most states, this means you must be at least eighteen years old.

• When you committed the offense: Often, a juvenile record can't be sealed until a certain length of time has passed since the end of the juvenile case. For example, the waiting period may be one, two, or

Whatever issues you need to confront or manage on your road to recovery, the process and pain is always worth the return of your life and health.

taking that step, nobody is going to punish you for it in the courts.

Your health is the most significant issue when dealing with addiction. Getting the help you need to get and stay sober and drug free should be your top concern. There may be relationships to rebuild and trust to regain and other hills to climb, such as getting back on track with school.

If there are legal issues to face as well, it's best to just own that and get it behind you, then move on and have a safer, healthier lifestyle.

THE WAR ON DRUGS HAS COMPROMISED TEENS

Although many laws and approaches to rehabilitation have the best of intentions for society, the so-called War on Drugs, which has existed in America for more than forty years, has had some negative consequences as well. Tony Newman is the director of media relations for the Drug Policy Alliance, and he describes the unintended outcomes of the war on drugs for teens in particular as the following:

> The defenders of the failed war on drugs say that we can't discuss alternatives to prohibition because it would "send the wrong message to the kids." Ironically, the drug war is a complete failure when it comes to keeping young people from using drugs.
>
> Despite decades of D.A.R.E. programs with the simplistic 'Just Say No' message, 50 percent of teenagers will try marijuana before they graduate and 75 percent will drink alcohol... Teenagers need honest drug education to help them make responsible decisions.

Newman also says the policies relating to the war on drugs have been bad for families: "The number of people behind bars on a drug charge in the U.S. has ballooned from 50,000 in 1980 to more than half-a-million today... Millions of people in the U.S. now have a father, mother, brother, sister, son or daughter behind bars on a drug charge."

New laws that emphasize recovery and reintegration to society without lasting punishment are a better approach to dealing with today's drug epidemic, particularly for youth.

Many consider the D.A.R.E. program's absitnence-only message to be short-sighted and advocate for a more realistic approach.

CHAPTER 6

MY PARENTS ARE ALSO ADDICTS. WHAT CAN I DO?

If you are struggling with a drug or alcohol addiction, it's important that you have the resources to support you in recovering and maintaining your sobriety and drug-free life. This book has discussed a lot of ways you can find the help you need, but much of the success rate for addiction recovery depends on the environment in which the recovering user lives.

Many people have parents who will provide the care and stability that a recovering addict needs, but what do you do if your parents also have a drug problem?

Will they be supportive of your desire to quit using drugs? Will they understand your desire to live drug-free, and the challenges that poses, especially early on in recovery?

It's difficult to stop using drugs if you are living in an environment in which drugs are present and easily accessible, and in which your own parents may actually be encouraging you to use drugs. Perhaps you have tried in the past to get your parents to stop using before you started taking drugs yourself.

If this is your situation, recovering will be more challenging for you, but that does not mean it's impossible. There are many resources

Being surrounded by other addicts, especially if they are your parents, can make addiction recovery extremely challenging. There are support groups specifically for children of addicts.

for recovering addicts whose parents are using drugs or for children who do not use drugs themselves but whose parents are addicts. This chapter will examine the effects a parent's drug or alcohol use can have on a child and where children of addicts can turn for help.

CONSEQUENCES FOR CHILDREN OF ADDICTS

There have been many studies researching the effects a parent's drug or alcohol addiction can have on their children, including research done by coaf.org. There are direct and indirect effects that can alter a child's development, emotionally and physically, and impact their social lives and chances for success at school.

According to an article published by *Pediatrics* in 1999, there has been a lot of research done into the effects of parental alcohol abuse on children. Less has been done on the impacts of other drug abuse, such as heroin or cocaine.

Children of addicts live in an unpredictable state. If your parent is using drugs, they are more likely to have legal, financial, relationship, and career problems that distract them from being more attentive, involved parents. You may frequently miss school or other important appointments because of your parent's drug use. You may have less money for necessities such as good food

A history of addiction can have a negative effect on a family for generations. Talk to your family members about any drug abuse that has occurred in your family.

Heavy metal legend Ozzy Osbourne was a drug and alcohol abuser for decades, and his daughter, Kelly, later had addiction problems of her own.

Kelly Osbourne, the reality television star and singer and daughter of heavy metal legend Ozzy Osbourne, revealed in her memoir *Fierce* that she struggled with an addiction to opiates that started at the age of sixteen.

She writes that she first took the prescription drug Vicodin when she was thirteen, following an operation to remove her tonsils. But three years later, she was offered a pill at a club by a friend, and quickly began using opiates recreationally. "I was relaxed, tingly and happy. The next morning, I called the guy and bought two or three pills for about $20," she writes.

When her mother, then a judge on television's *X Factor*, was diagnosed with breast cancer, Kelly started taking the tablets to cope, "I was trying to stay strong so I took Vicodin to hide the terrible sadness," she writes. "But by this point, I was waking up and emptying six Vicodin into my hand. Soon I was taking 50 pills a day. Most people would overdose on ten."

Kelly grew up in a rock-n-roll household with a father who struggled himself for years with drug and alcohol addiction. Still, when her parents saw photos online of Kelly buying opiates, they immediately responded to save their daughter. After three stays in rehab and one period in a psychiatric hospital, Kelly got control of her addiction. But even though she says the idea of a relapse makes her cry, she believes there is a "strong chance" it could happen if she doesn't keep focused on keeping clean.

KELLY OSBOURNE: "I WAS TAKING 50 PILLS A DAY"

If your parents are breaking the law and endangering you, it is possible legal authorities might get involved. This can often lead to children being removed from the home and placed in care.

Pamela McLucas has worked for twenty years as a substance abuse counselor at a children's home in Wichita, Kansas. According to her own informal statistics, 87 percent of the cases in which children were taken from their parent's home were related to substance abuse.

This can be frightening. Most children do not want to get their parents into trouble with the law and do not want to be placed in a children's home away from their family. But in cases where the home is not a safe or healthy environment, especially if you are also struggling with a drug addiction, it can be the best solution.

Consider your options. Is there a close friend you could stay with for

If your home does not feel like a safe place for recovery due to the drug use of other family members, find somewhere else to stay for a while if you can.

Following the drug-related death of singer Whitney Houston in 2012, *Tell Me More*, a program on National Public Radio hosted by journalist Michel Martin, focused on parents who are addicts and the effects addiction has on their children.

One of the guests was a Jennifer Brown, a mother of two teenagers who lives in Washington, DC. Brown shared her experience of falling heavily into alcoholism at age forty-two, following her divorce. Her children, then nine and twelve, didn't really notice much at first: "I was getting up at 6:00 in the morning and taking them to school and really still hungover—occasionally probably still a little drunk," Brown recalls. "But my children did not see that when they were very young and they did not grow up with it that way. I didn't start hiding alcohol until probably the last six months. But it was my children that saved my life."

She says eventually it was not possible to keep it from her children. "One Sunday my son showed up unexpectedly and I was passed out on the couch and there was a gallon of vodka sitting empty, sitting on the kitchen counter, and he was 14 years old. And I thought I'm not fooling him. I can tell him whatever I want but he's going to put it together, and I did not want that for him. It scared me to death. And I picked up the phone and very luckily I had a friend that I had known that had been in AA for 25 years, because I didn't really know what to do, and I called her. I had that access."

Now sober, Brown says she is very open with her children about her period of alcoholic drinking. She says they mostly notice that she is in a better mood and more relaxed, and they definitely prefer her sober.

One Mother's Recovery: "It Was My Children That Saved My Life"

American journalist and correspondent for ABC News and National Public Radio Michel Martin shed a light on the problem of parents who are also addicts on her radio program, *Tell Me More*.

a while or another family member with whom you can live?

If you are comfortable talking about this with your parents, you can explain to them that you need to focus on maintaining your sobriety. You can encourage them to stop using so you can move back home.

If you can't talk about this with your parents, seek another trusted adult—a family member, a teacher, a counselor, a doctor—who can help you have the conversation necessary to make arrangements for a better living situation.

WHERE CAN I TURN FOR HELP?

There are support groups you can contact to find help if your parents or guardians are struggling with drug or alcohol addiction. One such group, probably the most well-known, is Al-Anon, which provides "strength and hope for friends and families of problem drinkers."

There is a specific Al-Anon group for young adults, called Alateen, which provides support for teenagers whose parents are alcoholics. By joining Alateen and attending meetings, you can share experiences, strength, and hope with other teens in your situation, discuss difficulties, learn effective ways to cope with problems, encourage one another, and help each other understand the principles of the Al-Anon program.

Nar-Anon is a similar organization to help family members of drug addicts. It is nonreligious but spiritual in focus and based on twelve steps, similar to Alcoholics Anonymous and Al-Anon.

If you don't want to attend meetings or don't feel comfortable with the approach these organizations take, you can talk with a counselor or therapist about your experiences with your parent's addiction and how to limit the negative impact it can have on your life.

GLOSSARY

addiction The state of being hooked on a behavior or substance.

behavioral therapy A treatment that helps change potentially self-destructive behaviors.

counseling Professional guidance to help solve a difficult personal problem.

criminal record A criminal history that documents any arrests.

detox The process of ridding the body of harmful substances.

delinquent A young person who breaks the law.

dopamine A chemical that helps transmit signals to your brain, such as feelings of pleasure or reward.

drug A habit-forming medicinal substance.

inpatient care Medical treatment in which the patient stays for an extended time in the clinic.

juvenile court system A court system designed for underage offenders.

opioid Compounds that help reduce pain, such as prescribed pain killers.

outpatient care Medical treatment in which the patient visit the clinic for care but does not check in for an extended period of time.

possession A crime in which the offender is caught in possession of an illegal substance.

rehabilitation Medical treatment for addiction recovery.

relapse A term used when a person who has stopped taking a drug goes back to using.

sobriety The state of being free from the effects of drugs or alcohol.

stimulant Any food or drug that speeds up or stimulates the body and mind, such as caffeine.

substance abuse The act of using a drug beyond the prescribed dosage of a medical professional.

treatment Medical care for a disease, such as addiction.

treatment facility The place where treatment for addiction or another disease is given.

FOR MORE INFORMATION

Canadian Centre on Substance Abuse (CCSA)
75 Albert Street, Suite 500
Ottawa, ON K1P 5E7
Canada
(613) 235-4048
Website: http://www.ccsa.ca

The CCSA is an organization dedicated to the reduction of alcohol and drug abuse through education, policy reform, and research. It provides tools and resources designed to support schools, communities, and families in the prevention of drug use by adolescents.

Drug Abuse Resistance Education (DARE)
P.O. Box 512090
Los Angeles, CA 90051
(800) 223-DARE (3273)
Website: http://www.dare.com

DARE provides a curriculum taught by trained police officers that is designed to educate young people about drugs and crime.

Health Canada
Address Locator 0900C2
Ottawa, ON K1A 0K9
Canada
(866) 225-0709
Website: http://www.hc-sc.gc.ca/index-eng.php

Health Canada is the Canadian government's department responsible for public health. It offers resources regarding public health, drug abuse and addition, and law enforcement issues and policies.

Just Think Twice
Drug Enforcement Agency (DEA)
The U.S. Department of Justice
950 Pennsylvania Avenue, NW
Washington, D.C. 20530
(202) 307-1000
Website: https://www.justthinktwice.com

The DEA's Just Think Twice program provides facts about drug abuse and shares true stories about drug addiction from young adults.

Mentor Foundation USA
2900 K Street, NW, #501
Washington, D.C. 20007
(202) 536-1593
Website: www.mentorfoundationusa.org

Mentor Foundation USA is a part of the Mentor International foundation, which was started in 1994 under the auspices of the World Health Organization. Its American branch provides mentorship programs to help young people avoid drugs and excel academically.

National Council on Alcoholism and Drug
    Dependence, Inc. (NCADD)
217 Broadway, Suite 712
New York, NY 10007
(212) 269-7797
Hotline: (800) NCA-CALL (622-2255)
Website: www.ncadd.org

The NCADD operates with a network of health organizations dedicated to ending alcoholism and drug addiction, as well as their disastrous consequences on families and communities nationwide.

National Institute on Drug Abuse (NIDA) for Teens

National Institutes of Health

9000 Rockville Pike

Bethesda, MD 20892

(301) 496-4000

Website: http://teens.drugabuse.gov/about-us

NIDA for Teens is a project of the National Institute on Drug Abuse's outreach program for young adults.

Partnership for a Drug-Free Canada (PDFC)

Corus Quay

25 Dockside Drive

Toronto, ON M5A 0B5

Canada

(416) 479–6972

Website: http://www.canadadrugfree.org

PDFC provides information about commonly abused drugs, as well as tips parents can use to talk to their adolescents about drug use.

Phoenix House

2191 Third Avenue

New York, NY 10035

(888) 671-9392

Website: www.phoenixhouse.org

Phoenix House is a nonprofit treatment provider that offers drug rehabilitation services to teenagers, adults, and families. It offers affordable programs that combine education, social work, and mental health services to ensure lasting recovery.

Teen Challenge Canada
9340 Sharon Road
London, ON N6P 1R6
Canada
(877) 343-1022
Website: http://www.teenchallenge.ca/get-help/
    canadian-drug-crisis
Teen Challenge Canada is a twelve-month, faith-based, residential drug and alcohol rehabilitation program.

WEBSITES

Because of the changing nature of internet links, Rosen Publishing has developed an online list of websites related to the subject of this book. This site is updated regularly. Please use this link to access this list:

http://www.rosenlinks.com/411/drug

FOR FURTHER READING

Aronoff, Mark. *One Toke: A Survival Guide for Teens.* New York, NY: Porter House Publications, 2014.

Bakewell, Lisa. *Alcohol Information for Teens: Health Tips About Alcohol and Alcoholism.* Detroit, MI: Omnigraphics, 2009.

Covey, Sean. *The 7 Habits of Highly Effective Teens.* New York, NY: Touchstone, 2014.

Covey, Sean. *The 6 Most Important Choices You'll Ever Make.* New York, NY: Touchstone, 2006.

Jensen, Frances. *The Teenage Brain: A Neuroscientist's Survival Guide to Raising Adolescents and Young Adults.* New York, NY: Harper, 2015.

Ketchum, Katherine. *Teens Under the Influence: The Truth About Kids, Alcohol, and Other Drugs- How to Recognize the Problem and What to Do About It.* New York, NY: Ballantine Books, 2003.

Knapp, Caroline. *Drinking: A Love Story.* New York, NY: Dial Press Trade Paperback, 1997.

Lanksy, Sam. *The Gilded Razor: A Memoir.* New York, NY: Gallery Books, 2016.

Magill, Elizabeth. *Drug Information for Teens: Health Tips about the Physical and Mental Effects of Substance Abuse.* Detroit, MI: Omnigraphics, 2011.

Reznicek, Michael J. *Only You Can Save Your Kids: Teen Drug Use and How to Stop It.* CreateSpace Independent Publishing Platform, 2011.

Scheier, Lawrence M., and William B. Hansen. *Parenting*

and Teen Drug Use: The Most Recent Findings from Research, Prevention, and Treatment. New York, NY: Oxford University Press, 2014.

Sheff, David. Beautiful Boy: A Father's Journey Through His Son's Addiction. New York, NY: Mariner Books, 2009.

Sheff, David. Clean: Overcoming Addiction and Ending America's Greatest Tragedy. New York, NY: Eamon Dolan/Mariner Books, 2014.

Sheff, Nick. We All Fall Down: Living with Addiction. New York, NY: Little, Brown Books for Young Reader, 2012.

Steinberg, Lawrence. Age of Opportunity: Lessons from the New Science of Adolescence. New York, NY: Eamon Dolan/Mariner Books, 2015.

Volkman, Chris. From Binge to Blackout: A Mother and Son Struggle with Teen Drinking. New York, NY: NAL, 2006.

Wandzilak, Kristina. The Lost Years: Surviving a Mother and Daughter's Worst Nightmare. Santa Monica, CA: Jeffers Press, 2006.

Wolfsberg, Jeff. Message in a Bottle: Questions from Parents About Teen Alcohol and Drug Use. Wolfpack Publishing, 2012.

Youngs, Bettie B., and Jennifer Youngs. A Teen's Guide to Living Drug Free. Deerfield Beach, FL: HCI Teens, 2003.

Zailckas, Koren. Smashed: Story of a Drunken Girlhood. New York, NY: Penguin, 2006.

BIBLIOGRAPHY

American Academy of Experts in Traumatic Stress. "Effects of Parental Substance Abuse on Children and Families." Retrieved April 20, 2016. http://www .aaets.org/article230.htm.

CBSnews.com. "Teen Drug Abuse: 14 mistakes Parents Make." Retrieved April 5, 2016. http://www.cbsnews .com/pictures/teen-drug-abuse-14-mistakes-parents -make/2.

Clark, Josh. "How Addiction Works." HowStuffWorks. Com. Retrieved April 22, 2016. http://science .howstuffworks.com/life/inside-the-mind/human -brain/addiction.htm.

Daily Mail Reporter. "I Was Taking 50 Pills a Day: Kelly Osbourne Reveals How She Became Addicted to Opiates at 16." Mail Online, August 2009. http:// www.dailymail.co.uk/tvshowbiz/article-1209652/ Kelly-Osbourne-reveals-addicted-drugs--age-just-16 .html.

DrugAbuse.com. "30 Famous Actors and Actresses Who Have Battled Drug Addiction and Alcoholism." Retrieved April 8, 2016. http://drugabuse.com/30 -famous-actors-and-actresses-who-have-battled-drug -addiction-and-alcoholism.

DrugPolicy.org. "Protecting Youth." Retrieved April 28, 2016. http://www.drugpolicy.org/protecting-youth.

Eccles, Louise. "Singer Amy Winehouse died watching YouTube videos of herself after vodka binge, inquest hears." Mail Online, January 8, 2013. http://www. dailymail.co.uk/news/article-2258983/Amy -Winehouse-died-watching-YouTube-videos-vodka -binge.html.

Hartwell-Walker, Marie. "Teens and Drugs: What a Parent Can Do to Help." PsychCentral. Retrieved April 15, 2016. http://psychcentral.com/lib/teens -and-drugs-what-a-parent-can-do-to-help.

"How Addiction Hijacks the Brain." HelpGuide.org. Retrieved April 23, 2016. http://www.helpguide.org/ harvard/how-addiction-hijacks-the-brain.htm.

Johnson, Jeannette L., and Michelle Leff. "Children of Substance Abusers: Overview of Research Findings." *Pediatrics*, May 1999, vol. 103/issue supplement 2.

Martin, Michel. "When Parents Are Addicts, What Happens to Kids?" NPR, Tell Me More. Retrieved April 20, 2016. http://www.npr.org/2012/02/21/ 147193256/when-parents-are-addicts-what-happens -to-kids.

McNamara, Joseph. "Drug Laws Harm Teens More Than Pot Does." *New York Times*, December 19, 2011. http://www.nytimes.com/roomfordebate/2011/ 12/19/should-teenagers-get-high-instead-of-drunk/ drug-laws-harm-teens-more-than-pot-does.

Newman, Tony. "Nancy Reagan's Role in the Disastrous War on Drugs." *Huffington Post*, March 7, 2016. http://www.huffingtonpost.com/tony-newman/ nancy-reagan-war-on-drugs_b_9400628.html.

Partnership for Drug-Free Kids. "Top 8 Reasons why Teens Try Alcohol and Drugs." Retrieved April 9, 2016. http://

www.drugfree.org/resources/top-8-reasons-why-teens
-try-alcohol-and-drugs.

Pat Moore Foundation. "What My First Day in Drug Rehab Treatment Was Really Like." Retrieved April 15, 2016. https://www.patmoorefoundation.com/blog/what-my-first-day-drug-rehab-treatment-was -really.

Potter, Tim. "Substance Abuse a Top Reason Children are Removed from Homes." *Witchita Eagle*, May 17, 2014. http://www.kansas.com/news/article1143480 .html.

Rehabs.com "7 Addiction Myths About Teens and Their Parents." April 24, 2015. http://www.rehabs.com/7 -addiction-myths-about-teens-and-their-parents.

Scharff, Constance. "Seven Things to Expect When You Go to Rehab." *Psychology Today*, April 21, 2016.

Szalavitz, Maia. "Q&A: What Really Goes on In Drug Rehabs." Time.com, February 15, 2013. http:/ healthland.time.com/2013/02/15/qa-what-really -goes-on-in-drug-rehabs.

Theoharis, Mark. "Juvenile Drug Possession." CriminalDefenseLawyer.com. Retrieved April 10, 2016. http://www.criminaldefenselawyer.com/crime -penalties/juvenile/drug-possession.htm.

INDEX

ABOUT THE AUTHOR

Tracy Brown Hamilton is a writer and journalist based in Amsterdam. She has written several books for young adults on topics ranging from gay marriage to cyberbullying.

PHOTO CREDITS